LOONEY TUNES ANNUAL 1998

£6.99

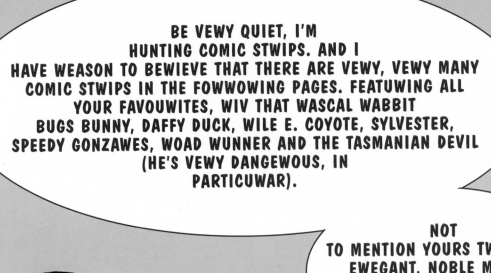

Contents

7

13

Oh, ROMEYBLECH, ROMEYBLECH, WHERE €@$%#% FORE ART THOU, ROMEYBLECH?
WHACK
WHACK
WHACK
DENY THY %#@¢ FATHER AND REFUSE THY €%#$@ NAME, AND TAZ NO LONGER BE A HUH?!
THAT'S CRACKS IT, YOU MANGY MUTANT! I'M CUTTING YOU OUTTA THE SCRIPT FOR GOOD!
WHACK
KRACK
SWACK
THAT'LL SHOW YOU! COME DOWN HERE AND DUKE IT OUT LIKE A--
KRRRRACKKK
--ON SECOND THOUGHT, CAN I TAKE A RAIN CHECK ON THAT?
YIPE!

15

Writer: Dana Kurtin Penciller: Walter Carzon Inker: Scott McRae
Letterer: Bob Pinaha Colorist: Jo Meugniot

Porky Pig Activities

E-BUH-BUH WELCOME TO P-PORKY P-PIG'S SPOT THE DEE-E-BUH-DEE-DEE-DIFFERENCE! THE PAIR OF P-UH-BUH-BUH-PICTURES ON THESE P-PAGES HAVE TEN DEE-E-BUH-DEE-DEE-DIFFERENCES BETWEEN THEM.

CAN YOU SPOT ALL THE DEE-E-BUH-DEE-DEE ... ER... BITS THAT DON'T MATCH?

ANSWERS ON PUH-E-PUH-PUH-EH-BUH-PAGE 110.

16

Writer:Dave King Penciller:Nelson Luty Letterer:Teresa Davidson Inker:Horacio Ottolini
Coloristst:Grace T. Bland

19

20

PORKY! HEY, PORKY!

E-bu-buh... HI, DAFFY!

OLD BUDDY, OLD PAL! TELL ME YOU REMEMBER WHAT I DID WITH MY LOTTERY TICKET! P-P-PUHLEAZE!

G-GOSH!

OH, G-GEE, I D-DON'T KNOW! MAYBE I CAN REMEMBER AND M-MAYBE I CAN'T! I'M G-GETTING ALL FUH-FLUSTERED!

MAYBE THIS'LL LOOSEN UP YOUR BRAIN, YOU MORON!

DON'T YOU REALIZE MY LIFE OF MEANINGLESS, WEALTHY INACTIVITY IS AT STAKE HERE!

IT'S N-NO G-GOOD! I CAN'T R-REMEMBER!

ARRGH! YOU'RE USELESS! REMIND ME TO FORGET YOU WHEN I'M WEALTHY!

I CAN'T WASTE TIME HANGING AROUND WITH A LOSER LIKE YOU ANY LONGER!

THANK G-GOODNESS!

21

WA·15S

WORDS! TAZ LOOOVE WORDS!

Taz'll eat anything, even words. But can you help him find the characters hidden in the jumble below?

Words can go forwards, backwards, top-to-bottom, side-to-side and even diagonally.

Answers on page 110.

Here are the hidden words. But can you find them?

Daffy Duck
Bugs Bunny
Wile E. Coyote
Elmer Fudd
Speedy
Sylvester
Porky Pig
Yosemite Sam
Tweety
Taz

M	Y	S	K	L	A	W	G	D	J	T	D
R	S	W	S	A	P	I	B	E	T	A	Y
S	T	W	I	L	E	E	S	O	F	D	O
P	P	C	O	Y	O	T	E	F	U	I	S
B	O	L	A	H	H	W	Y	C	A	A	E
U	R	M	N	A	E	E	K	E	Z	E	M
G	K	M	V	E	S	E	P	O	T	M	I
S	Y	L	V	S	A	T	E	R	Q	P	T
B	P	S	K	P	A	P	E	D	J	T	E
U	I	W	E	A	P	S	A	B	T	R	S
N	G	E	E	N	P	P	A	Z	O	S	A
N	D	R	L	A	L	A	I	N	T	A	M
Y	E	L	E	L	M	E	R	F	U	D	D

Lettering: Bob Pinaha Inking: Khato Colorist: Tom Ziuko

Writers: Dana Kurtin and Dan Slott Pencillor: Pablo Zamboni

29

BUGS'S CARROT CHAOS!

Bugs is in trouble now! One of the pieces of string leads to his favourite carrot, but if he picks the wrong one it could be curtains! Can you find which piece of string is the right one?

Answer on page 110.

34

MUNCH MUNCH

I JUST **LOVE** SNOWMAN SEASON.

WA·49·5

MULTI-BUNNY BLUES

WB 385

BUT I DON'T *TASTE* GOOD-- HONEST! I'M ALL *STRINGY* AND FULL OF *BONES!*

TAZ LOOOOOVE STRINGY BONES!

Writer: Bobbi JG Weiss   Penciller: Horacio Saavedra   Inker: Ruben Torreiro   Letterer: Bob Pinaha   Colorist: David Tanguay

AND I'M *TOUGH* LIKE OLD SHOE LEATHER!

TAZ LOOOOOVE SHOE LEATHER!

OKAY, JUST *HOLD IT* A SECOND!

SCREEECH

40

ROOARRGH fnargle BLEECH

CLIK

Holed Up

Writer: David Weiss   Penciller: Horacio Saavedra   Inker: Ruben Torreiro   Letterer: Steve Haynie   Colorist: Jo Meugniot

WB283

43

44

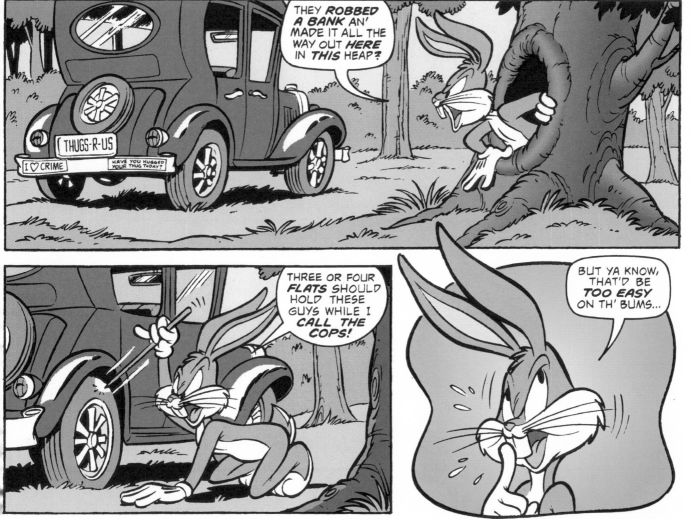

THEY *ROBBED A BANK* AN' MADE IT ALL THE WAY OUT *HERE* IN *THIS* HEAP?

THREE OR FOUR *FLATS* SHOULD HOLD THESE GUYS WHILE I *CALL THE COPS!*

BUT YA KNOW, THAT'D BE *TOO EASY* ON TH' BUMS...

AN' BESIDES, I JUST CAN'T LEAVE THAT *MR. BIG* RUNNIN' AROUND LOOSE!

ANYWAY, THOSE JOIKS *DESOIVE* WHAT'S GONNA HAPPEN TA THEM!

HEY, GUYS! I FOUND A VINTAGE CARROT JUICE *SO GOOD* WE OUGHTA TAKE IT TO *MR. BIG,* HIMSELF!

MR. BIG? WHO'S THIS MR. BIG?

48

YOU KNOW, YOU GUYS ARE REALLY *LUCKY* I'M *BETWEEN JOBS* ...I MEAN *ON VACATION!*

I'M IN *BIG DEMAND!* LOTSA STUDIOS ARE JUST *WAITIN'* TO *NAIL* ME WITH A *CONTRACT!*

I KIN *BELIEVE* IT! *I'M* DREAMIN' OF PUTTIN' OUT A *CONTRACT* ON YOU MYSELF!

SO... WHAT DO YOU WANT ME TO DO? *ROMEO? HAMLET? JULIUS SNEEZER?*

DON'T LET 'EM KNOW *I* TOLD YA, DAFFY--BUT THESE GUYS ARE *REALLY* INTO *GANGSTER STUFF!*

THEY ARE? Y'KNOW, I DO A *GREAT* BOGART!

WHAT KIN I *SAY?* YA GOTTA WOIK WITH THE MATERIAL YA GOT!

Y'KNOW, SWEETHEART, *THIS* COULD BE THE START OF A *BEAUTIFUL RELATIONSHIP...*

SAY, FELLAS--DON'T LOOK *NOW*, BUT I THINK WE'RE BEIN' *FOLLOWED!*

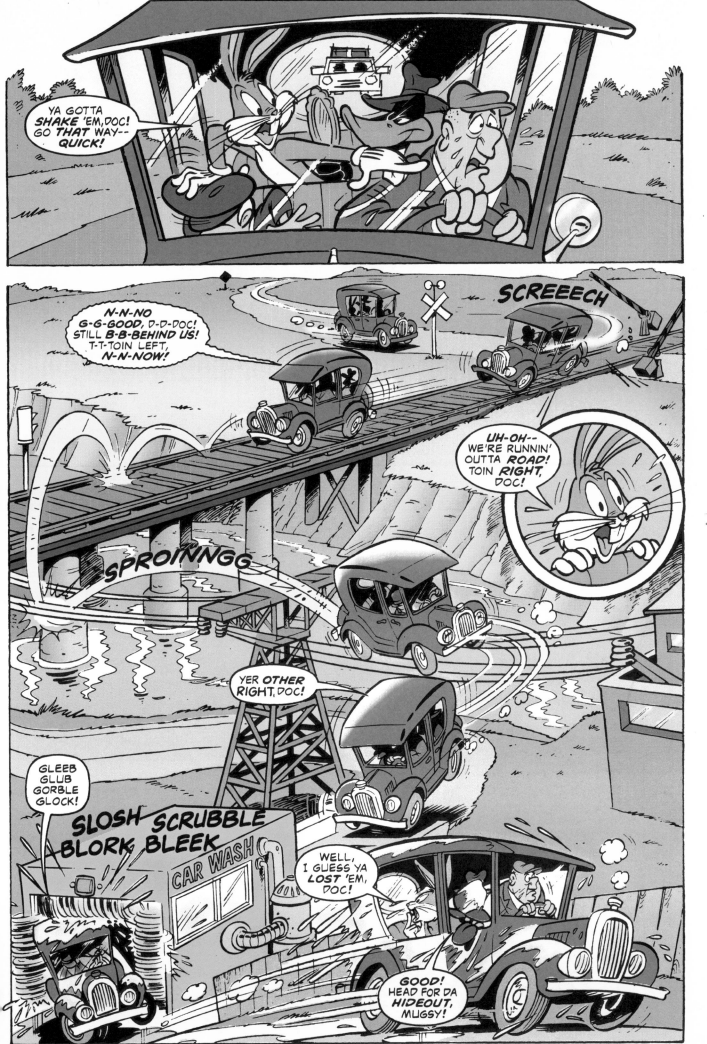

51

WELL, DAFFY, I...

DAFFY *WHO?* I'M "BEAKY" DUCK-- THE *TOUGHEST* QUACKER ON THE EAST SIDE!

I DON'T TAKE *NOTHIN'* FROM *NOBODY*--LEAST OF ALL GOONS THAT LEAVE THEIR *LUNCH* LAYIN' AROUND!

LUNCH, EH? WELL, I SUPPOSE *ANYTHING* CAN COME IN HANDY!

JUNK YARD

FINALLY --SAFE AT *HOME!*

WHAT WAS *DAT?!*

OH, NO-- AN *AMBUSH!* THEY *GOT* ME!

I'M *DONE FOR,* FELLAS...DON'T LET ME ÷KOFF÷ HOLD YA *BACK!* GO ON *WITHOUT* ME...BEFORE THEY ÷KOFF÷ GET *YOUSE* TOO!

DON'T *WORRY, PAL!* WE'LL *GET* THE DIRTY RATS THAT DID YOU *IN!*

SLAM

WHAT A BUNCHA *MAROONS!*

NOW, WHAT CAN I FIND TA MAKE THEM JOIKS' LIVES *REALLY* MISERABLE?

JUNK YARD

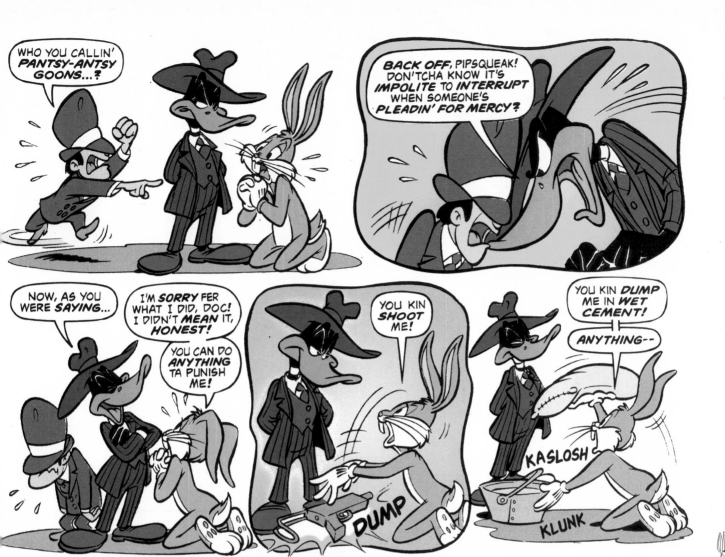

57

59

MAKE A LOONEY TUNES MOBILE

You can have your favourite Looney Tunes characters getting in your way all the time with this great LOONEY TUNES MOBILE!
Just follow the simple instructions below.

1.

CUT OUT THE PICTURES

2.

MAKE A HOLE AT THE TOP OF EACH PICTURE AND THREAD SOME STRING THROUGH

3.

PLACE TWO COAT HANGERS AT RIGHT ANGLES LIKE THIS, THEN HOLD THEM TOGETHER WITH STICKY TAPE

4.

USE MORE TAPE TO HANG EACH CHARACTER FROM THE MOBILE

5.

THEN LEAVE IT SOMEWHERE TO ANNOY YOUR PARENTS

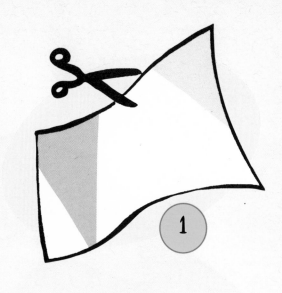

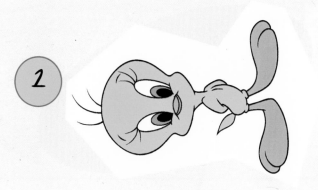

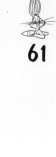

61

62

63

64

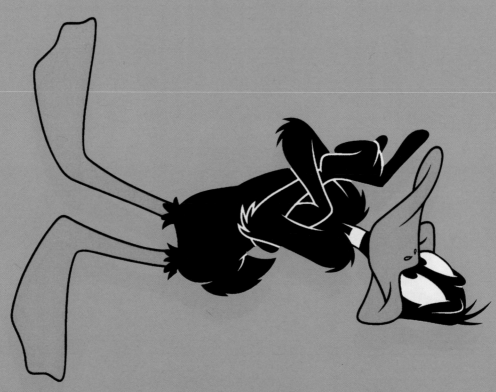

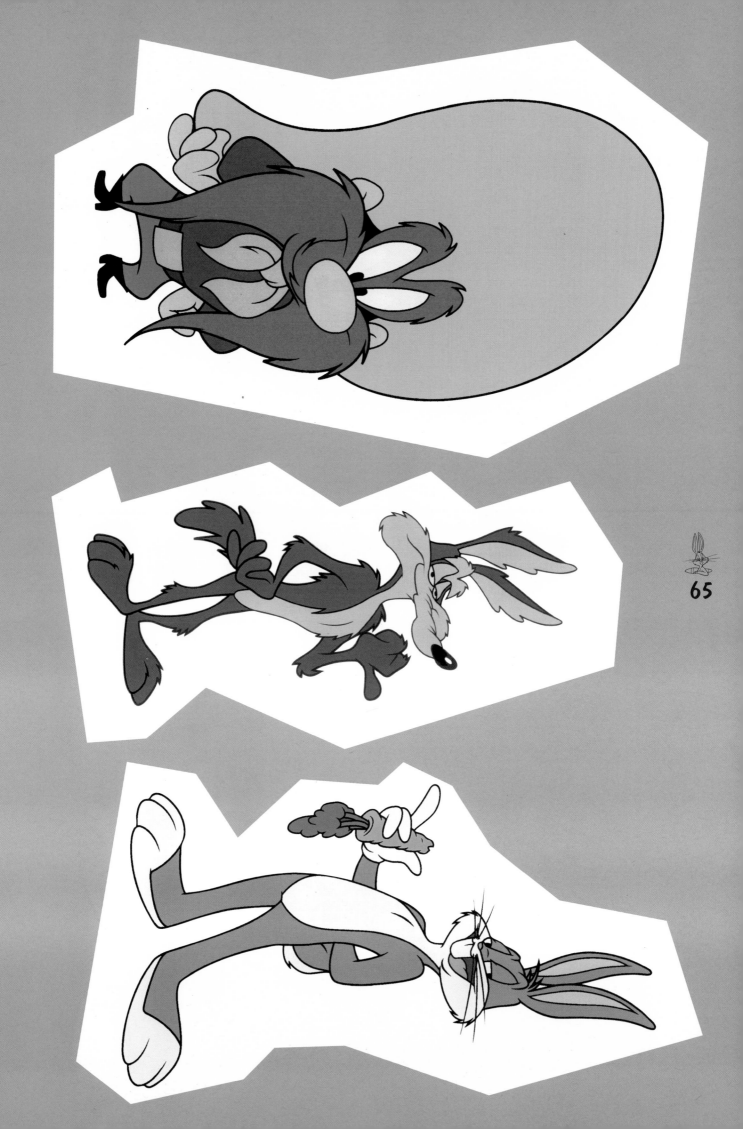

65

66

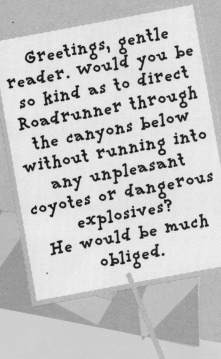

Greetings, gentle reader. Would you be so kind as to direct Roadrunner through the canyons below without running into any unpleasant coyotes or dangerous explosives? He would be much obliged.

ROAD RUNNER MAZE

67

THE OPEN ROAD

IT TAKES A SAINT TO MAKE A COMPLAINT

Writer: David Cody Weiss **Penciller:** Horacio Saavedra **Inker:** Ruben Torreiro **Letterer:** Lorina Mapa **Colorist:** Jo Meugniot

68

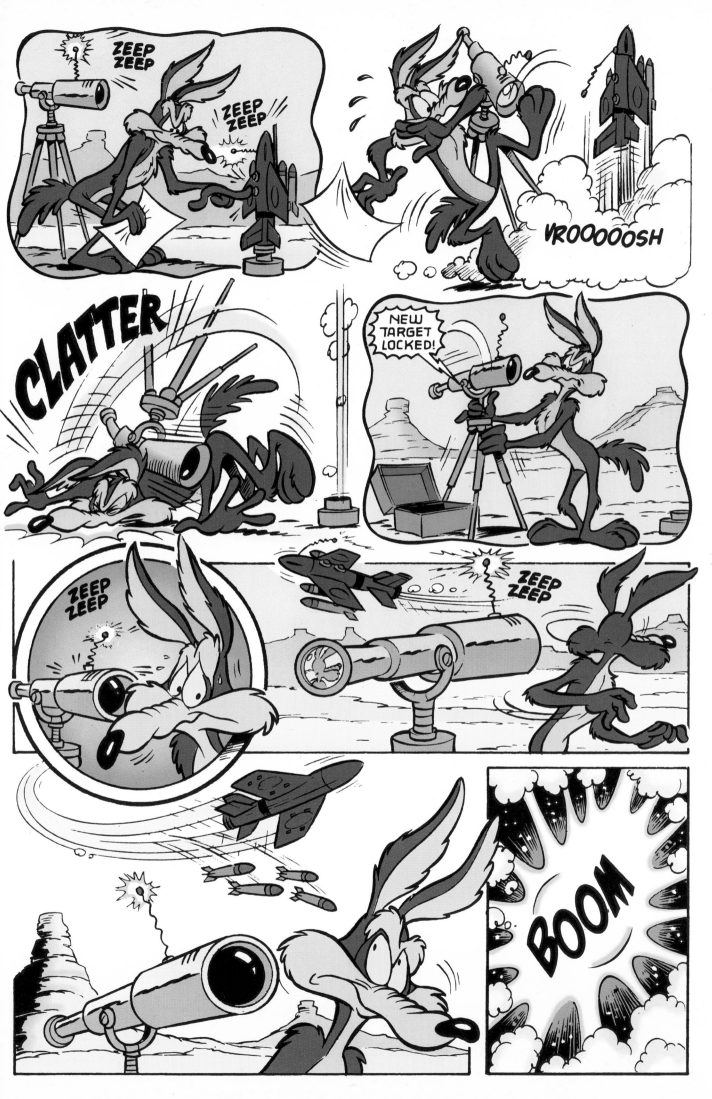

GUARANTEED IF NOT SATISFIED, CALL 1-800-OUCH

THANK YOU FOR CALLING ACME. IF YOU ARE AN INCOMING CALL, PLEASE PRESS 1.

IF YOU WISH TO CONNECT TO THE COMPLAINT DEPARTMENT, PLEASE PRESS 3...

...IF YOU WEIGH MORE THAN 180 PLEASE PRESS 5...

...IF NOT, PLEASE PRESS 12...

BIP BIP BIP

...IF THE MOON IS IN LEO, PRESS 451...

BIP

BIP BIP BIPPITY BIP BIP

...IF ONE-EYED JACKS ARE WILD, PRESS 7737...

...THANK YOU! PLEASE WAIT ON THE LINE AND YOUR CALL WILL BE ANSWERED BY THE FIRST AVAILABLE OPERATOR.

YOU HAVE REACHED THE *CLIENT DISSATISFACTION DEPARTMENT.* THANK YOU FOR HOLDING.

WE *VALUE* YOUR COMMENTS. TO FILE A COMPLAINT, PLEASE LEAVE YOUR MESSAGE AT THE SOUND OF THE *CLICK.*

CLICK!

HUMMMM...

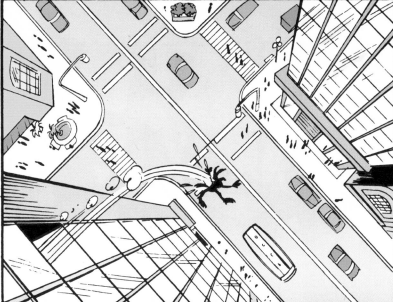

75

INSTRUCTIONS

Thank you for purchasing this BOOK™. We, the publishers at ACME, hope that it will bring you many hours of entertainment.

TROUBLESHOOTING

If your BOOK™ is unreadable. Have you tried turning it the other way? The 'spine' should be facing left and the front cover should be at the front. If your BOOK™ is still unreadable, ensure that you are not sitting in the dark, or trying to read the BOOK™ while it is still in the 'off' position (i.e. closed). The publishers accept no responsibility for external distractions beyond their control, such as your parents making you go to bed, your siblings stealing the BOOK™, or the dog eating it.

MANUFACTURERS' WARRANTY

Remember to read this page of the BOOK™ first. If you have already read the previous 75 pages, you will have activated the ACME patent self-destruct mechanism, designed to keep this BOOK™ from falling into the hands of coyotes, rabbit hunters and bird-eating cats. You have been warned. This BOOK™ will explode in ten seconds.

Writer: Jack Enyart   Penciller: Horacio Saavedra   Inker: Ruben Torreiro   Letterer: Agnes Pinaha   Colorist: Jahrome Youngker

77

SCREEE

PLINK

FLING

THUNK

CRUNCH

WB 481

Writer: Jack Enyart   Penciller: Horacio Saavedra   Inker: Ruben Torreiro   Letterer: Bob Pinaha   Colorist: Tom Zuiko

83

84

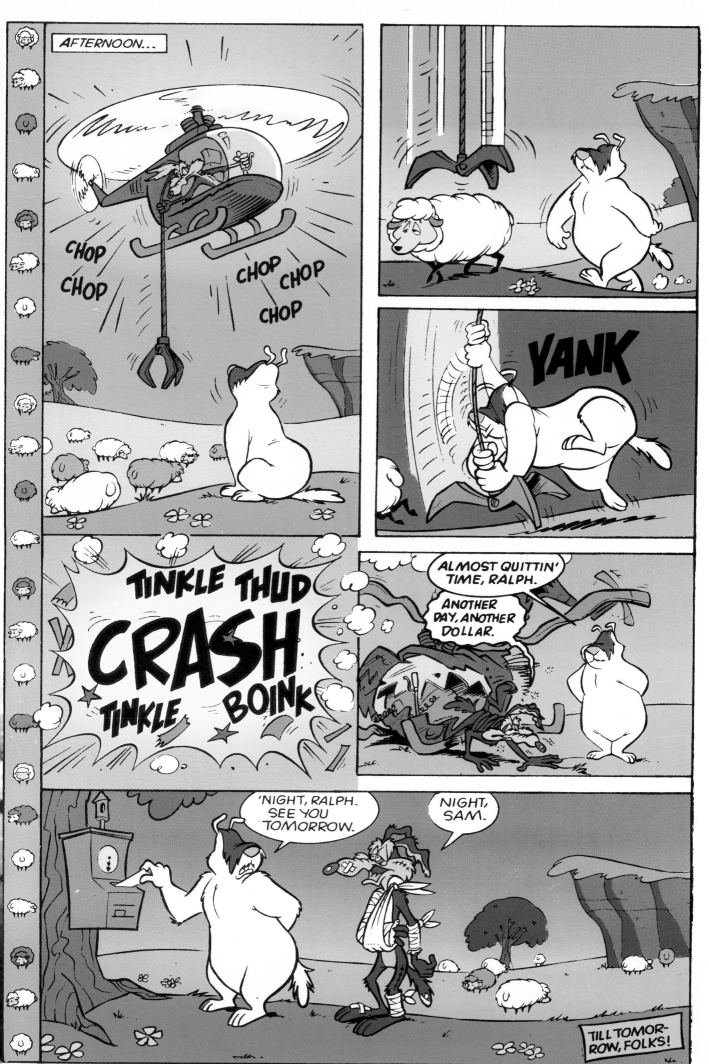

AH-SAY AH-SAY
AH-HANG ON JUST A COTTON PICKIN' MINUTE
THEYAR! AH-SAY AH'VE BEEN WAITIN' AHLL
THIS TIME TO SEE MAHSEYULF IN THIS HEYAH
BOOK AND AH HAVEN'T BEEN IN A SINGLE ONE
OF THEM THEYAH COMIC
STRIPS!

KNOW YER ENEMY

SO
NOW AH'VE
GOT MAH SAY, SOME
OF THE INDIVIDUALS AH-SAY
INDIVIDUALS ON THESE PAGES ARE OUR
FRIENDS,
BUT THIS IS MAH CHANCE
TO WARN ALL THOSE FELLOW BIRDS OUT
THEYAR ABOUT OUR ENEMIES.

DO,
AH-SAY DO YOU KNOW WHO
I MEAN? THE ANSWERS ARE
ON PAGE, AH-SAY
PAGE 110.

86

THIS HEYAH ANIMAL COULD BE YER PET, BUT
HE'S GOT WIYULD RELATIONS LIKE LIONS AND
TIGERS. HE SPENDS HIS TIME CHASIN' A LITTLE
BIRD CALLED TWEETY, BUT IF HE EVUH CAME
NEAR ME HE'D GET A TASTE OF LEGHORN'S
ANGER, AH CAN TELL YUH! COZ FOGHORN
LEGHORN AIN'T NO CHICKEN! DO YAH HEYAH ME?

THIS HEYAH ANIMAL'S WHAT WE CALL A PRAIRIE
WOLF. LIKE A SMALL WOLF THAT YER FIND ON THE
PRAIRIES OUT HEYAH IN THE STATES. HE LIKES
CHASIN' THEM THEYAR ROAD RUNNERS, BUT HE
AIN'T NEVER GONNA CATCH ONE. COZ THEM THEYAR
ROAD RUNNERS IS LIKE A FAST LEGHORN.

AH SAY WATCH OUT FOR THIS HEYAH ANIMAL COZ
HE'S THE MOST DANGEROUS. HE'S A HUMAN BEING
WHO LIKES HUNTIN' ALL SORTS OF CRITTERS,
'SPECIALLY RABBITS AND A CERTAIN KINDA DUCK.
LOOK OUT FOR THE SMOOTH PELT, THE LARGE GUN
AND THE REEDICKERLESS, AH-SAY REEDICKERLESS
SPEECH IMPEDIMENT.

WE BIRDS AIN'T EVEN SAFE IN THAT THEYAH
AUSTRALIA WHEN THIS THEYAH CRITTER'S ON
THE LOOSE. HE'LL EAT JUST ABOUT
ANYTHING, AND THAT INCLUDES ANY
FOGHORN LEGHORN THAT AIN'T FAST ON THE
DRAW!

Writer:Dana Kurtin and Dan Slott Pencillor:Nelson Luty Lettering:John Costanza Inking:Horacio Ottolini Colorist:Jahrome Youngker

94

96

97

TWEETY'S JOIN THE DOTS

Something is creeping up on Tweety. Can
you find out what it is by joining the dots?

99

Writer:Dana Kurtin and Dan Slott   Penciller:Nelson Luty   Letterer:John Costanza   Inker:Horacio Ottolini   Coloristst:Jahrome Youngker

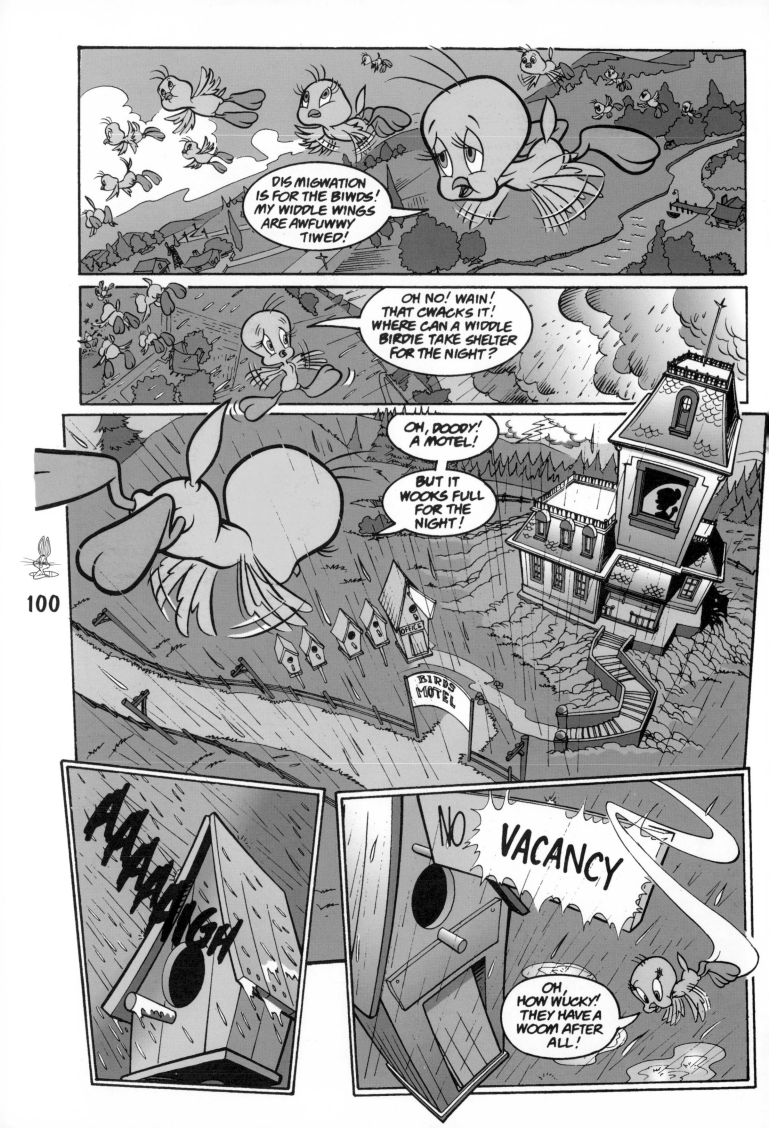

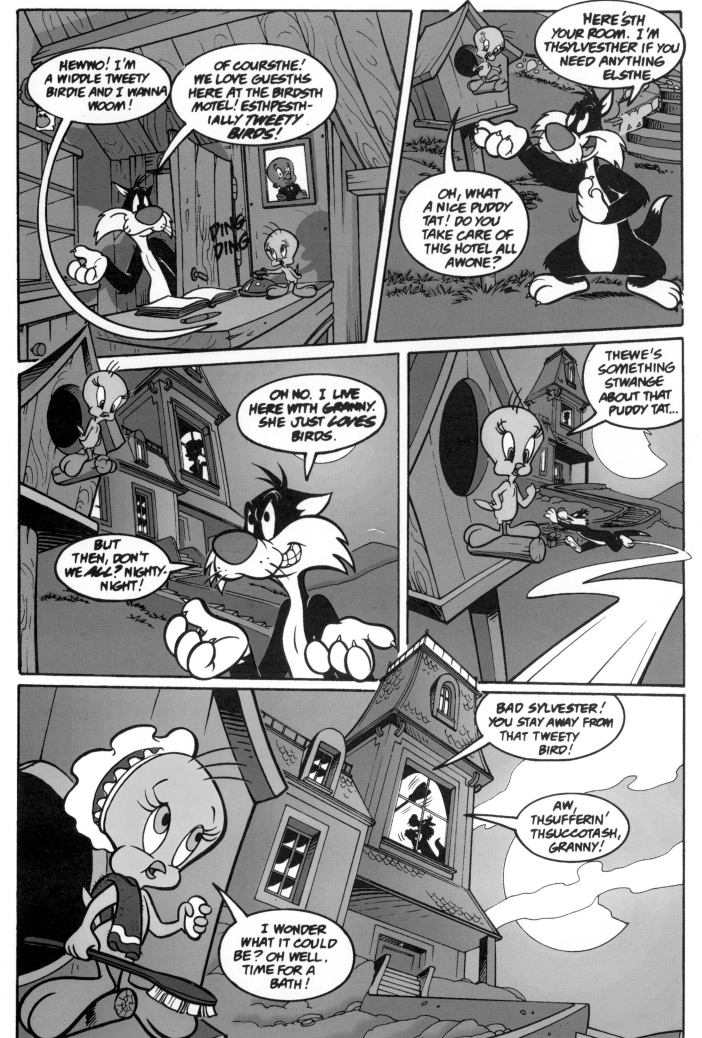

101

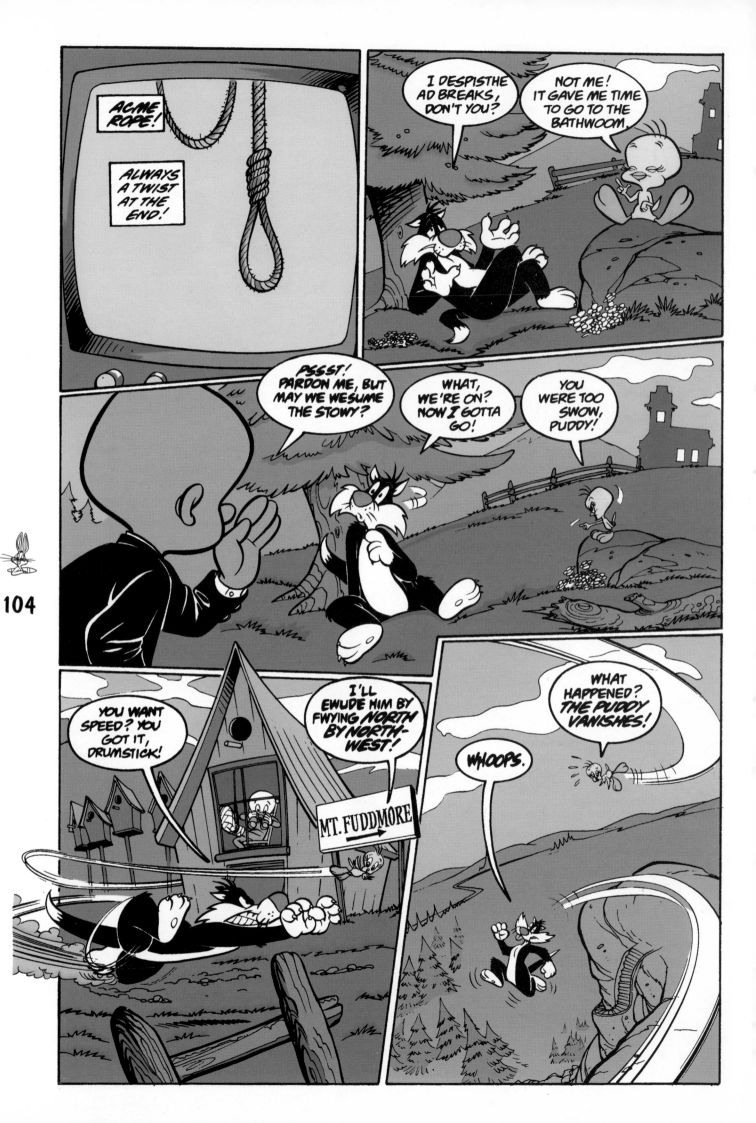

105

106

TWUWY A SAD CASE, DON'T YOU AGWEE? FACED WITH DEWICIOUS BIWDIES DAY IN, DAY OUT, THE CAT SNAPPED-- BECOMING PSYLVESTER.

HIS "GWANNY" PEWSONALITY WAS CWEARWY AN ATTEMPT TO THWART HIS CWUEL, TWISTED DESIWES.

THERE HE IS!

WITH MY ADVANCED EXPEW-IENCE IN PSYCHIATRY--

ACH! DAT IS KVITE ENOUGH, MR. FUDD!

FORGIVE ZIS INTRUSION. ZIS IS NOT ALFWED HITCHFUDD, BUT ONE OF MY PATIENTS!

HIS REAL NAME IS ELMER J. FUDD, MILLIONAIRE. HE OWNS A MANSION UND A YACHT. DIS "HITCHFUDD" PERSONALITY IS MERELY UN ILLUSION!

MUCH LIKE ZIS ENTIRE SHTORY WAS MERELY A HALLUCINATION OF HIS FEVERED BRAIN!

EXCEPT FOR ACME ROPE, OF COURSE -- BUY ZOME NOW! AS YOU CAN ZEE, IT ALWAYS HAS A TWIST AT ZE END!

The End

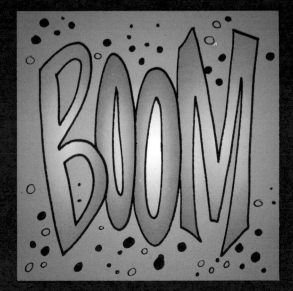

ANSWERS

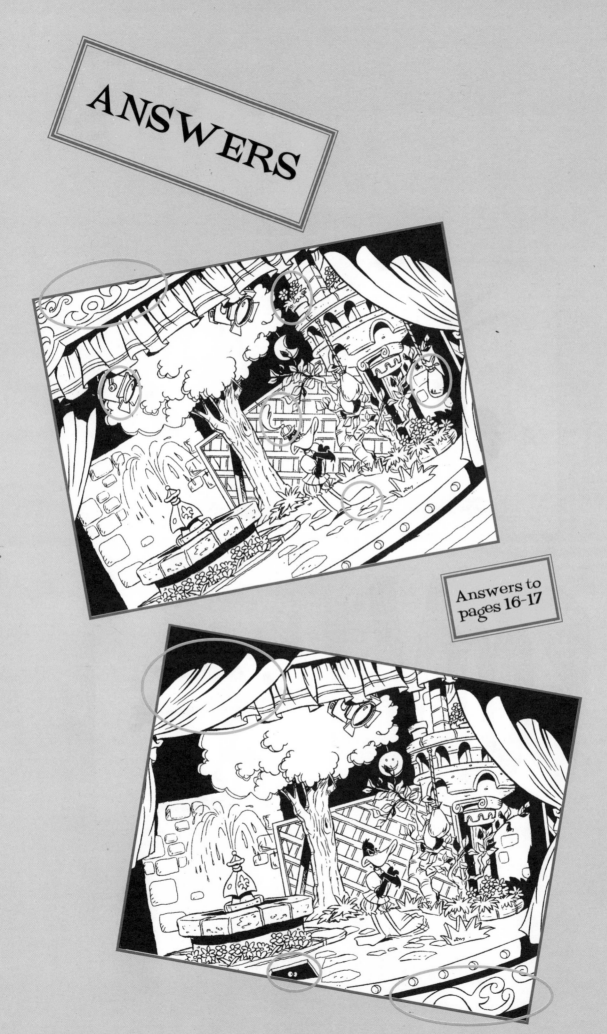

Answers to
pages 16-17